THE LIBRARY OF CONSTELLATIONS™

Pisces

Stephanie True Peters

The Rosen Publishing Group's
PowerKids Press™
New York

For Brendan and Eric, superstar brothers

Published in 2003 by The Rosen Publishing Group, Inc.
29 East 21st Street, New York, NY 10010

First Edition

Editors: Natashya Wilson, Veronica Vergoth
Book Design: Michael Caroleo, Michael Donnellan, Michael de Guzman

Photo Credits: Cover, p. 4 © John Sanford and David Parker/Science Photo Library/Photo Researchers; back cover, title page, p. 8 Bode's Uranographia, 1801, courtesy of the Science, Industry & Business Library, The New York Public Library, Astor, Lenox and Tilden Foundations; pp. 6, 7, 12 © Stapleton Collection/CORBIS; p. 9 (left) © Mimmo Jodice/CORBIS p. 9 (right) © Adam Woolfitt/CORBIS; pp. 11, 15, 20 (lower left) by Michael de Guzman; p. 16 © Digital Vision; p. 19 Todd Boroson/NOAO/AURA/NSF; p. 20 © John Chumack/Photo Researchers.

Peters, Stephanie True, 1965–
Pisces / Stephanie True Peters.— 1st ed.
p. cm. — (The library of constellations)
Includes bibliographical references and index.
Summary: Discusses the constellation Pisces, its location among the stars, myths about its origin, and its presence in the zodiac, as well as basic concepts of astronomy.
  ISBN 0-8239-6166-4 (library binding)
1. Pisces (Constellation)—Juvenile literature. 2. Zodiac—Juvenile literature. [1. Pisces (Constellation) 2. Astronomy. 3. Zodiac.] I. Title. II. Series: Peters, Stephanie True, 1965– . Library of constellations.
  QB803 .P43 2003
  523.8—dc21

                                                                    2001004858

Manufactured in the United States of America

Contents

The Fish in the Sky

For thousands of years, people have seen different shapes outlined by the stars in the night sky. Each shape made of stars is called a constellation. The constellations are named for the people, the animals, or the objects they are thought to look like. People imagine that the constellation Pisces, also called the Fish, looks like two fish whose tails are tied together by ribbons or cords. The stars in Pisces form a shape that looks like a crooked V turned on its side. The fish are at either end of the V. The ribbons that are attached to their tails join at the point of the V. Pisces is near other constellations that share its water theme. Capricornus the Sea Goat, Aquarius the Water Bearer, and Cetus the Whale are all near Pisces.

Fun Facts

No one knows how long ago people began to group stars into constellations. One known Greek work that mentions them dates from before 350 B.C.

The top line of Pisces's V is known as the northern fish.
The bottom line is known as the western fish.

How to Find the Fish

Pisces can be seen in the Northern **Hemisphere** in the fall and in the Southern Hemisphere in the spring. To find Pisces in the Northern Hemisphere, face north and find the Big Dipper. Trace a line from the two stars of the Big Dipper's outer bowl upward until you find **Polaris**, the North Star. Above Polaris is the *W* shape of the constellation **Cassiopeia**. Look above Cassiopeia and turn around to face south. Beyond Cassiopeia is the Great Square, part of the constellation **Pegasus**, the Flying Horse. It is high in the southern sky. Below the Great Square is the Circlet, the ring of stars that forms one fish of Pisces. The Circlet is the easiest part of Pisces to see, because there are not many other stars around it. Trace the line of stars to the left of the Circlet to the point of the *V*, then trace Pisces's second line of stars upward to find the second fish.

In this picture, the fish of Pisces surround the back of Pegasus, the Flying Horse, at the top of the circle. The constellations Andromeda and Aries are below the bottom fish.

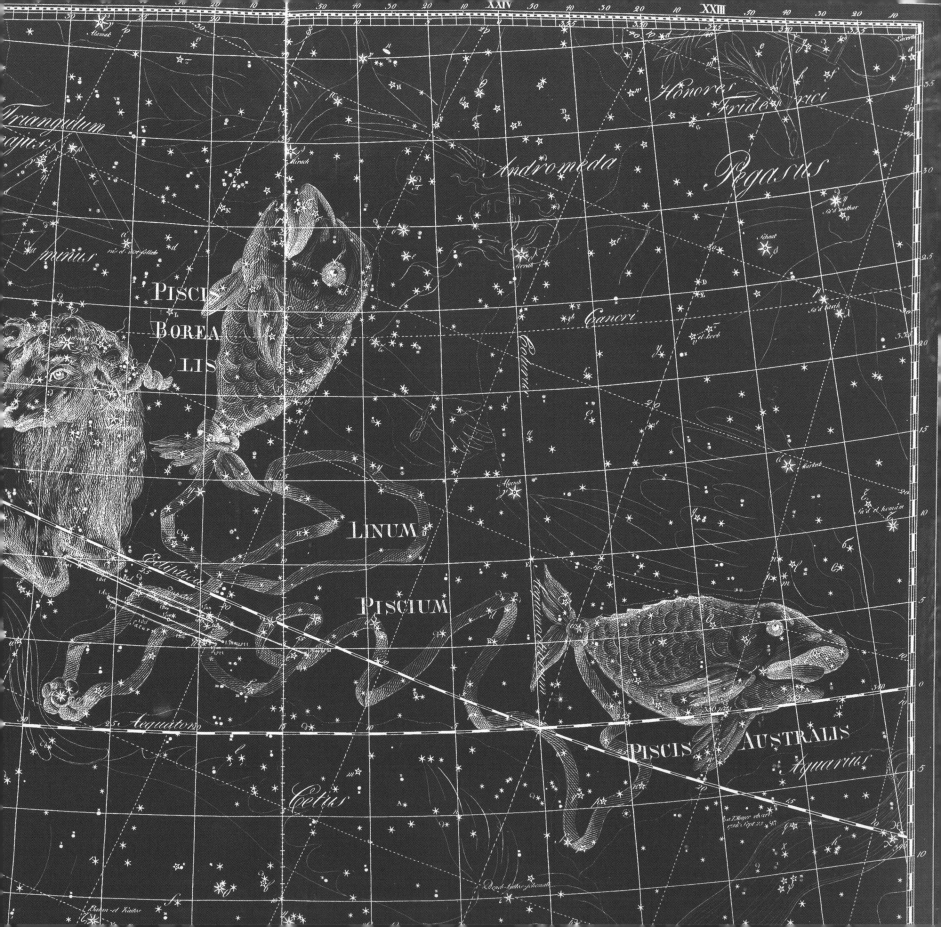

The Pisces Myth

According to Greek myth, the fish of Pisces represent the goddess **Aphrodite** and her son **Eros**. The ancient Greeks told the story of a huge, terrifying monster named Typhon. Typhon had wings, serpents for thighs, and the head of a donkey. He was so large that when he spread his wings, he blocked the Sun. Fiery rocks shot out of his mouth. Typhon attacked Mount Olympus, home of the Greek gods. The gods fled. Each god turned into an animal to escape. Aphrodite and Eros turned into fish. They tied their tails together so they wouldn't lose each other as they swam away. **Zeus**, the king of the gods, stopped Typhon by throwing Mount Aetna on top of him. When Mount Aetna, an active volcano in Italy, erupts, the myth says that Typhon is trying to break free.

In fall, Pisces can be seen in the Northern Hemisphere in this position, with its V opening upward in the sky.

The Zodiac and Astrology

Pisces is one of the constellations of the **zodiac**, the group of 12 constellations that seem to make a ring around Earth. The other 11 constellations are Aquarius, Capricornus, Sagittarius, Scorpius, Libra, Virgo, Leo, Cancer, Gemini, Taurus, and Aries. These constellations are the basis of **astrology**, the ancient belief that the movements of the stars and the planets affect life on Earth. Many people believe that the position of the zodiac constellations and the planets on the day a person is born determines what his or her life will be like. Daily **horoscopes**, or readings of the stars and the planets, are thought to forecast the type of day a person will have. Today people can find their horoscopes in many places, including in newspapers, in magazines, and on the Internet.

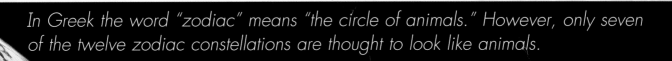

In Greek the word "zodiac" means "the circle of animals." However, only seven of the twelve zodiac constellations are thought to look like animals.

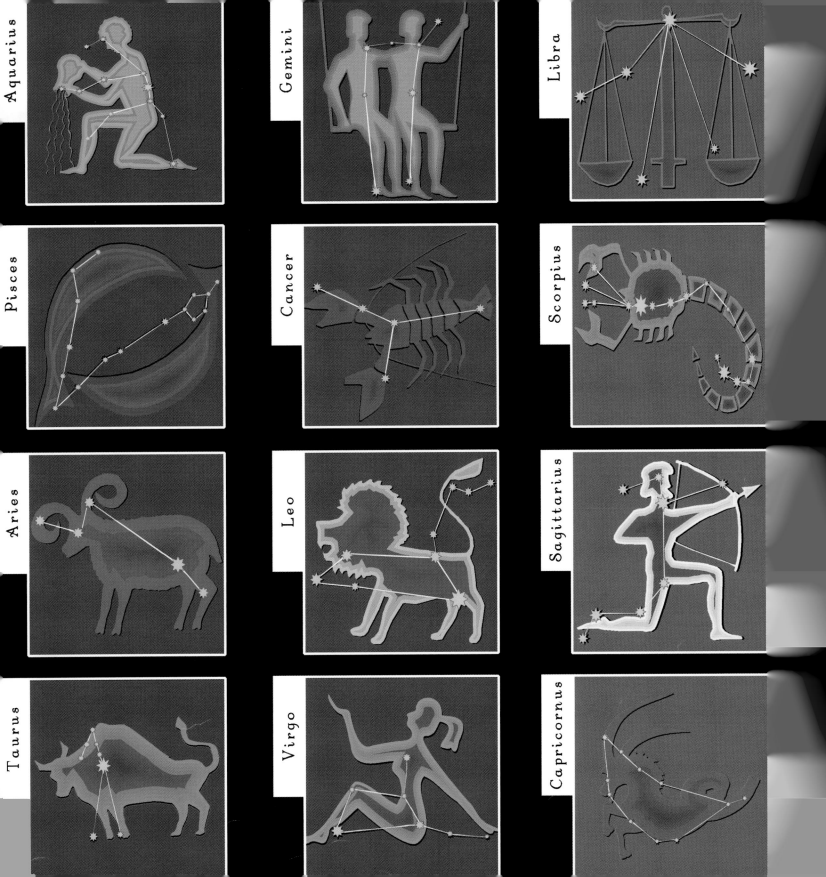

Aquarius

Gemini

Libra

Pisces

Cancer

Scorpius

Aries

Leo

Sagittarius

Taurus

Virgo

Capricornus

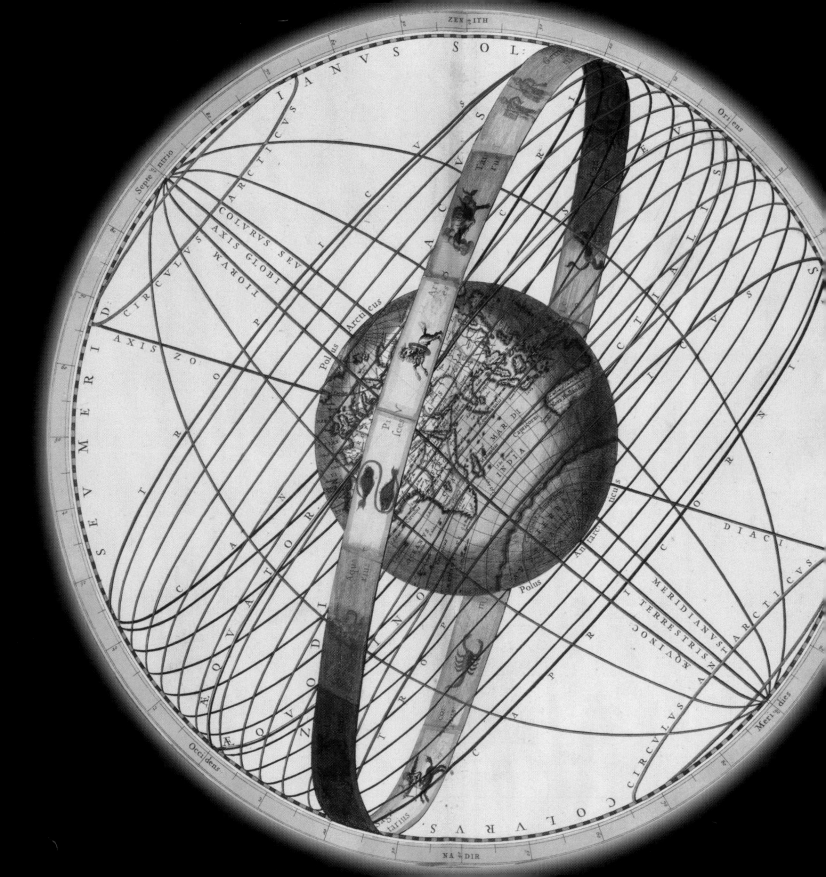

The Path of the Sun

Imagine that Earth is surrounded by a glass ball dotted with the stars and other heavenly bodies seen in space. This ball is called the **celestial sphere**. The 12 zodiac constellations line up in a circular path around the celestial sphere. As one year passes, the Sun appears to move along the path through all 12 zodiac constellations. It stays in each constellation for one month. The line of the Sun's apparent path is called the **ecliptic**. The Sun does not actually move along the ecliptic. It is Earth's yearly circle, or orbit, around the Sun that makes the Sun appear to move. All the planets in our solar system follow the ecliptic as they orbit the Sun. One way that **astronomers** learn about the movement of the planets is by tracking the planets as they pass through the different zodiac constellations.

From Earth the zodiac constellations seem to form a ring in the night skies. Every month a new constellation comes into view, and an old one disappears.

The First Day of Spring

Another imaginary line circles the celestial sphere. It is called the **celestial equator**. The celestial equator circles the celestial sphere at the same angle that Earth's **equator** circles Earth. Twice every year, the Sun's apparent path on the ecliptic crosses the celestial equator. The points where the ecliptic and the celestial equator cross are called **equinoxes**. The Sun reaches one equinox on about March 21 each year. This equinox occurs in Pisces, near the Circlet. It is called the **vernal equinox**. It marks the first day of spring in the Northern Hemisphere. The second equinox marks the beginning of fall in the Northern Hemisphere. It occurs on about September 21 each year. On the days of the equinoxes, the hours of daytime and nighttime are equal in both hemispheres.

As Earth circles the Sun, the Sun's apparent position moves along the ecliptic. When the Sun's position passes through Pisces on the ecliptic, the vernal equinox occurs.

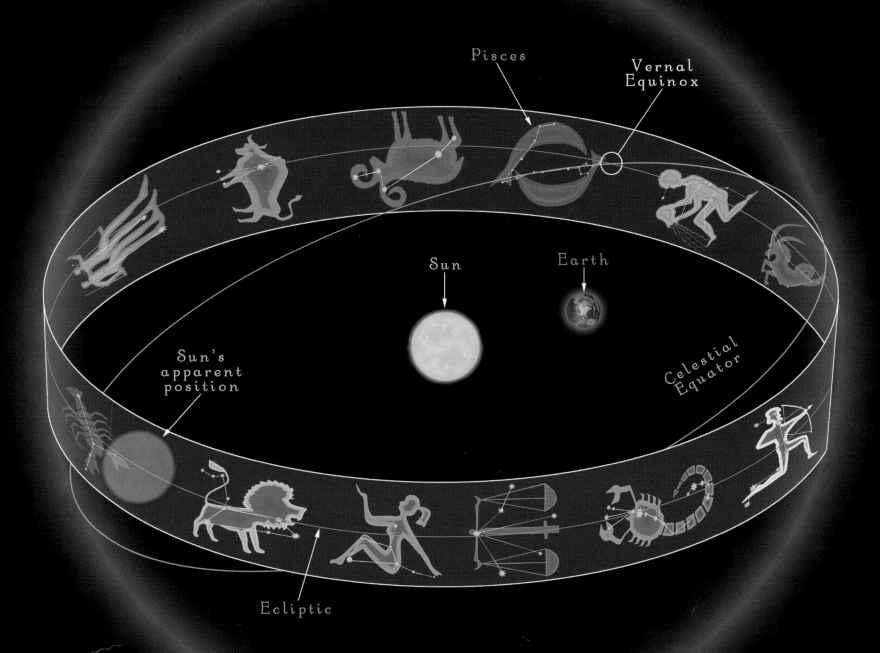

Pisces

Vernal Equinox

Sun

Earth

Sun's apparent position

Celestial Equator

Ecliptic

Starlight

If you stare at the stars in Pisces for a while, you may notice that each star looks a little different. Many things affect how a star's light will look in the night sky. Brighter stars might be younger than fainter stars. They might be closer to Earth. They also might be bigger than fainter stars. Astronomers measure how bright stars look from Earth in **magnitude**. Stars with low magnitude numbers are the brightest. From Earth a star named Sirius is the brightest star in the night sky. Its magnitude is less than 0! The stars in Pisces are not very bright. The brightest star has a magnitude just a little less than 4. Starlight also comes in different colors. A star's color depends on how old the star is. The youngest stars are blue. Stars' colors change from blue, to white, to yellow, to orange, and then to red, as they grow older. The change in color happens over billions of years. The stars in Pisces are many different colors, including blue, yellow, and red.

When you first look up at the stars on a night like this, they might all look white. As you gaze awhile, you will start to see that the stars are different colors.

Galaxy M74

A galaxy is a cluster of millions or billions of stars. Earth belongs to the Milky Way galaxy. The universe contains many other galaxies. They are so far away that from Earth they look like small, blurry dots in the night sky. Galaxy M74 can be found near the middle of the line of stars that forms Pisces's upper fish. M74 is about 35 million **light-years** away and can be seen only through a powerful telescope. A light-year is the distance light travels in one year, about 6 trillion miles (10 trillion km). Like the Milky Way, M74 is a spiral galaxy. Spiral galaxies look like pinwheels of stars.

M74 got its name from the man who discovered it, astronomer Charles Messier. Messier was born in Badonviller, France, in 1730. He started studying the stars when he was 14 years old. In 1760, Messier began to list the objects he found in the sky. M74 was the seventy-fourth object on Messier's list.

Charles Messier added this beautiful spiral galaxy, now called M74, to his famous list sometime between August and December 1780.

Al Rischa

Center

The Double Star Knot

The star that marks the point of Pisces's *V* is called alpha Piscium, or Al Rischa. *Al rischa* is Arabic for "the knot." In the Pisces myth, Al Rischa is the place where the ribbons tied to the fish's tails are knotted together. It is the brightest star in Pisces.

Al Rischa is a double star. Its two stars orbit around a common center. Although its stars look faint from Earth, Al Rischa is about 100 times brighter than the Sun. Al Rischa looks faint because it is about 98 light-years away from Earth. The Sun is less than 1 light-year away from Earth!

Fun Facts

Stars shine because they are very hot. The surface of the Sun is about 9,900°F (5,482°C). The surface of a new star can be as hot as 90,000°F (49,982°C)!

The two stars that make up Al Rischa take about 933 years to make a complete circle around their common center.

Van Maanen's Star

Another interesting star in Pisces is Van Maanen's Star. It is located just below the middle of the line of stars that forms Pisces's lower fish. This star is named for the astronomer Adriaan van Maanen, who discovered it in 1917. Van Maanen's Star is one of the closest stars to us. It is about 14.4 light-years, or 86.4 trillion miles (137 trillion km), away from the Sun. It is very small for a star. It is a little smaller than Earth, and it is dim. Small, dim stars are called white dwarves. They are some of the oldest stars in the sky. Van Maanen's Star is so dim that it can be seen only through a telescope. Whether you have a telescope or not, there are many beautiful stars and other objects to see in Pisces, and in all the night sky.

Glossary

Aphrodite (af-ro-DY-tee) The Greek goddess of love, from Greek mythology.

astrology (uh-STRAH-luh-jee) The belief that the stars and the planets affect life on Earth.

astronomers (uh-STRAH-nuh-merz) People who study the Sun, the Moon, the planets, and the stars.

Cassiopeia (kas-ee-uh-PEE-uh) Queen of Ethiopia, mother of Andromeda, and wife of Cepheus, from Greek mythology.

celestial equator (suh-LES-tee-ul ih-KWAY-tur) The imaginary line that marks the middle of the celestial sphere.

celestial sphere (suh-LES-tee-ul SFEER) The imaginary ball, of stars, planets, the Sun, and the Moon, that surrounds Earth.

ecliptic (ee-KLIP-tik) The path the Sun appears to follow around Earth each year; home of the zodiac constellations.

equator (ih-KWAY-ter) The imaginary line that circles Earth an equal distance from the North and South Poles.

equinoxes (EH-kwih-noks-ez) The days of the year when the hours of day and night are equal.

Eros (ER-ohs) The son of the Greek goddess of love, Aphrodite. Eros is also known as Cupid.

hemisphere (HEH-muh-sfeer) Half of a sphere, or half of Earth.

horoscopes (HOR-uh-skohps) Astrological readings that predict the future based on the positions of heavenly bodies.

light-years (LYT-yeerz) The distance light travels in one year, about 6 trillion miles (10 trillion km).

magnitude (MAG-nih-tood) The measurement of a star's brightness.

Pegasus (PEH-guh-suhs) A horse with wings, Greek mythology.

Polaris (poh-LAR-is) The North Star, or the Pole Star.

vernal equinox (VER-nuhl EH-kwih-noks) The point where the ecliptic and the celestial equator meet on about March 21, the first day of spring.

Zeus (ZOOS) King of the Greek gods and goddesses, from Greek mythology.

zodiac (ZOH-dee-ak) The 12 constellations that seem to circle Earth.

Index

Web Sites

To learn more about constellations and Pisces, check out these Web sites:
www.enchantedlearning.com
www.hubblesite.org
    www.lhs.berkeley.edu/starclock